## SCHIRMER PERFORMANCE EDITIONS

# MOZART
## 15 INTERMEDIATE PIANO PIECES

## Edited and Recorded by Elena Abend

To access companion recorded performances online, visit:
**www.halleonard.com/mylibrary**

Enter Code
7196-8612-8861-8018

On the cover:
*Mozart's Family*
by Johann Nepomuk della Croce
(1736-1819)

© The Art Archive/CORBIS

ISBN 978-1-4234-2035-4

# G. SCHIRMER, Inc.

DISTRIBUTED BY

HAL•LEONARD®
CORPORATION
7777 W. BLUEMOUND RD. P.O. BOX 13819 MILWAUKEE, WI 53213

www.musicsalesclassical.com
**www.halleonard.com**

# CONTENTS

3    **HISTORICAL NOTES**

4    **PERFORMANCE NOTES**

**Andantino in E-flat Major, KV 236 (588b)**

12

**Minuet in F Major, KV 1d**

13

**German Dance in C Major, KV 605, No. 3**

14

**Minuet in F Major, KV 5**

16

**Contradance in G Major, KV 269b**

18

**Minuet in F Major, KV 6 (II)**

20

**Adagio for Glass Harmonica, KV 356 (617a)**

22

**Funeral March for Signor Maestro Contrapunto, KV 453a**

24

**Allegro in F Major, KV Anh. 109b, No. 1 (15a)**

26

**Minuet in G Major, KV 15y**

28

**Rondo in C Major, KV 334 (320b)**

30

**Piece for Clavier (Klavierstück), KV 33B**

32

**Contradance in D Major, KV 534**

34

**Gavotte in F Major, KV Anh. 10 (299b)**

36

**Rondo in F Major, KV 15hh**

39

42    **ABOUT THE EDITOR**

The price of this publication includes access to companion recorded performances online, for download or streaming, using the unique code found on the title page. Visit **www.halleonard.com/mylibrary** and enter the access code.

# HISTORICAL NOTES

## WOLFGANG AMADEUS MOZART (1756-1791)

Many of the pieces in this volume are works that Mozart wrote as a child, and some are among his very earliest compositions. It is fascinating to imagine what early boyhood must have been like for the young Wolfgang Amadeus Mozart. His precocious musical talent was already evident to his father, Leopold, when Wolfgang was as young as four years old. By age six, he was a harpsichord virtuoso and was composing his own music. Leopold, a violinist and composer, was his children's sole teacher, instructing them in all subjects, including music. Wolfgang's earliest original compositions were likely written with his father's assistance, or were heavily edited by his father, though they reveal extraordinary talent.

Leopold was an enterprising man and sought to share the considerable talents of his children with the world. He arranged various concert tours for the family, some lasting as long as three years. They traveled throughout the courts of Europe, with Wolfgang and his older sister, Nannerl, performing on the harpsichord, and Leopold playing the violin. Wolfgang ultimately spent about ten years of his childhood traveling on these concert tours.

The three Mozarts dazzled the courts of Europe, especially young Wolfgang. Aside from playing prepared pieces, he performed a number of tricks, such as playing with the keyboard covered by a cloth and sight-reading difficult music. He also exhibited his astounding memory by playing back pieces that he had heard only once. These skills further expanded in adulthood, when Wolfgang routinely improvised elaborate pieces at the keyboard during concert performances.

Many of the hosts for the family's concerts were kings and queens, including the Empress Maria Theresa and her daughter Maria, who later became Marie-Antoinette of France. Maria Theresa was so delighted with the children's performance that she sent them a set of tiny court clothes as a gift.

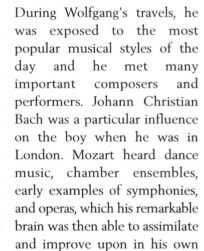

During Wolfgang's travels, he was exposed to the most popular musical styles of the day and he met many important composers and performers. Johann Christian Bach was a particular influence on the boy when he was in London. Mozart heard dance music, chamber ensembles, early examples of symphonies, and operas, which his remarkable brain was then able to assimilate and improve upon in his own works. Even as a child he was a prolific composer, writing concertos, symphonies, sonatas, and operas by the age of 13. Today, his numerous solo piano sonatas and piano concertos remain important staples of the piano repertoire.

—*Susanne Sheston*

# PERFORMANCE NOTES

Wolfgang Amadeus Mozart composed the keyboard pieces in this volume during the period from 1761, at age six, until 1791, the year of his death. The early pieces are so sophisticated that it is nearly inconceivable that they are the work of a child, and the later works show Mozart at the height of his compositional powers. Though the pieces are brief, they are all fully conceived compositions, unfailingly elegant in Mozart's innate understanding of voice leading and harmony.

From a pedagogical perspective, the pieces in this publication can serve many purposes. Music of the Classical era, and particularly Mozart's music, lays bare the technique of a pianist much more than a Chopin waltz or a Rachmaninoff prelude. The music has a leanness of texture that exposes any unevenness or technical shortcomings of the performer. Mozart's pieces are perfect compositions that beg to be performed perfectly. Playing them can teach (among other skills) restraint, lightness of touch, and beauty of tone. The challenge is to find the shape and style of each little piece.

Unlike Clementi's *Sonatinas*, Op. 36, which were written specifically as teaching pieces, many of the early works in this collection were essentially the young Wolfgang's composition lessons, which were reviewed by his father Leopold. They come from either *Nannerl's Notebook*, a book of compositions Mozart's father Leopold kept for Wolfgang's older sister's piano study, or Mozart's *London Notebook*, a composition notebook Wolfgang kept during the family's performing tour to that city in 1764-65. Very few dynamic or articulation indications are given in urtext sources. (Mozart gave very few such indications in his later works as well, trusting performers to understand the style, typical of the time.) The purpose of this edition is to show elements of style through editorial additions in the score. Any added markings are placed in brackets. There is a line somewhere between printed recommendations in an edition for the purpose of style and coaching a performance in the score. Listening to the companion CD, particularly with the guidance of a teacher, may allow a student to observe many more details of articulation and phrasing than could be notated.

These pieces can lead a student naturally to some of Mozart's easier piano sonatas, such as the Sonata in C Major, KV 545, or Beethoven's easier piano sonatas, such as the two sonatas of Op. 49.

## Articulation and Phrasing

The piano in Mozart's time was still in its infancy, and had a much looser, more nimble key action. This instrument was conducive to producing a delicate lightness of touch that should be emulated in performances on modern pianos. Additionally, Mozart composed many of his early works for harpsichord and clavichord, both of which have a very limited dynamic range. As a result, clear articulation and phrasing were needed to bring performances to life. Fingering is a vital aspect of finding this sparkle in your playing. Most of the fingering recommendations were made in service to the articulation of a phrase, be it legato, staccato, or portato (see below for explanation of these terms). Articulations in this edition are suggested to bring the style of these pieces to the fore. Fingering has been chosen for the average hand; you may decide to use different fingerings that are more comfortable for a particular player's hands. Regardless of the fingering, it is important to remember that in Classical repertoire, fingering *is* articulation. The choice of fingering will have a significant impact on the clarity of the articulation and phrasing. For instance, notice the fingering in measure 3 of the "Rondo in C Major" and how it requires the pianist to lift before the printed slur.

*Rondo in C Major, KV 334 (320b), m. 3*

Three basic articulations are found in this volume:

## LEGATO

Legato is the Italian word for "bound." Legato playing is usually shown with slurs and requires a smooth connection of the notes with no separation between them.

The notes are "bound" together. In this style of music, in a series of slurred notes, there are slight lifts (or breaths) between the slurs.

## STACCATO

Staccato (Italian for "detached") is indicated by a dot over a note. These notes should be shortened considerably from their printed duration. It is important to note that staccato does not mean accented or punched, but simply means short and detached.

## PORTATO

Portato is an articulation that lies somewhere between legato and staccato. It requires less separation than true staccato, but is not to be performed smoothly, as in legato playing. It is often notated with slurred staccato markings.

In this edition, there are many instances when a passage might not have any articulation marked at all.

*Minuet in F Major, KV 1d, mm. 17-20*

This and many other similar passages are effectively performed with a portato articulation. It is crucial to understand that portato is the default articulation of Classical style. True staccato and legato are deliberate choices to spell the otherwise constant portato approach. Many pianists encourage blandness in playing music of this period with constant legato playing when portato is the better stylistic choice. It gives the music character and contrast, and produces clarity of texture.

# Dynamics

As mentioned above, many pieces in this volume were likely composed for the harpsichord or clavichord, which were limited in their dynamic range. It is important to keep this in mind when performing these works on the modern piano. The clavichord had an especially intimate quality of sound that could never come close to matching the power of today's pianos. Classical restraint is essential to performing the dynamic indications with integrity, even on a modern piano with more dynamic range. The bracketed dynamics are editorial suggestions.

# Pedaling

Mozart did not write pedal indications for any of the pieces in this volume. The damper pedal did not start to be used in pianos until very late in the 18th century, after these pieces were written. While pedal should not be arbitrarily banned from performances of this music, it is essential that when the pedal is used, that it is with the utmost discretion. Most, if not all, of the pieces in this volume can be performed satisfactorily without using the damper pedal at all. Removing the crutch of the pedal will force your fingers to find clear, elegant intentions, which the pedal often blurs when not used with taste. We indicate pedal suggestions for the "Funeral March for Signor Maestro Contrapunto" to assist in sustaining a rich *forte* dynamic. One might also use a little pedal in the "Adagio for Glass Harmonica" (see example) to help with legato phrasing, but it should never impede the clarity of the harmony or the melodic line. Experiment with depressing the pedal only one-half or one-quarter of the full depth to avoid choppiness and unwanted extra noise from the dampers.

*Adagio for Glass Harmonica, KV 356 (617a),*
*mm. 1-4*

# Ornamentation

Appoggiaturas, acciaccaturas, and trills abound in this music and add to its grace and style. Appoggiaturas are indicated by grace notes without a slash through them, and are generally performed in a lyrical manner, on the beat in the Classical era, not before it. Acciaccaturas (possibly from the Italian *acciaccare*, to crush) are indicated by grace notes with a slash, and normally only appear in pieces with a quick tempo. They should be played quickly, "crushed" in just before the beat, almost simultaneous with the principal note. In this edition the execution of all ornaments is notated above the music staff at the relevant points. Trills generally start from the note above in music of this period, often with a concluding *Nachschlag* (termination).

# Tempo

In many pieces in this collection, there were no tempo indications written by Mozart. We have placed tempo suggestions in brackets for those pieces that did not have such indications. Additionally, a suggested metronome marking is indicated at the beginning of each piece. These markings are suggestions only. Tempo is a particularly subjective aspect of interpretation, with no two pianists likely to choose the exact same tempo for a piece. But how does one chose an appropriate tempo? This is a challenging question that faces students and teachers. With pieces that are dances (minuets, contradances, etc.), knowing something about how that dance is performed will assist in choosing the proper tempo and style. From a purely technical point of view, you can isolate the most difficult section of a piece, or the section with the most moving notes, to determine which tempo will work best for that passage, then apply that to the entire piece. Be sensitive to an appropriate aesthetic of Classical restraint in choosing a tempo. Find a tempo that will bring the organic elegance of these pieces to life. Extremes of tempo should be avoided, and steadiness is crucial. Unlike Chopin's music, with its fluidity and rubato, varying the tempo in a Mozart piece, except at rare and deliberate points, destroys the essence of the music. Mozart wrote the following in a letter to his father from Augsburg on October 24, 1777: "Nannette Stein [a young musical prodigy from Augsburg] will never acquire the most essential, the most difficult and the chief requisite in music, which is, time, because from her earliest years she has done her utmost not to play in time…Everyone is amazed that I can always keep strict time."[1] Only very occasionally do we suggest a *poco rit.* or a fermata in this edition.

# Style

Style is the most important element in a performance of Mozart's music, and in many ways is the most difficult to define. These little pieces hold importance and interest for students and concert artists. They are complete, satisfying works. Their style is the fusion of dynamics, articulation, and tempo together with Classical restraint and technique. Mozart's style has a lively elegance that comes from the crystalline texture of his music, along with his supreme gift as a melodist. Mozart is quoted in *The Reminiscences of Michael Kelly, 1826*, saying that "Melody is the essence of music."[2] He valued this quality above all others in music. His phrases beg to be sung. Mozart was, after all, one of the greatest vocal composers. Phrasing is key in performing his music, understanding how each phrase builds and eventually tapers to its conclusion, and interacts and leads into the next phrase.

Don't confuse slurs with phrasing. Slurs are about articulation, not broader shape. Imagine listening to an actor in a play who never observed the commas or periods written in the script. Their performance would be, at best, bland and at worst, completely unintelligible. You can think of slurs as clauses within a larger musical sentence, the phrase. As you can see in the example above there are many small slurs contained within one overarching phrase. This concept of building to a peak and releasing can be applied to many pieces and phrases in this book. This should not be an exaggerated effect. Exaggeration is not a part of this style. Even when there are *subito* changes in dynamic, they are performed in a more restrained manner than would be expected in Romantic music.

## Minuets

Mozart composed many minuets in his early years, several of which are included in this edition. The minuet (sometimes also spelled menuet) is a restrained, complex, and elegant dance, which has its origins in France It has a stately, aristocratic quality and was most popular from 1650 until 1800. Dance often inspired art music, particularly in the Baroque era when entire suites of dances such as bourrées, minuets, musettes, polonaises, and sarabandes were composed by J. S. Bach and others. The minuet was the only Baroque dance to survive past 1750. Not surprisingly, after the French Revolution and the death of the aristocracy, the minuet faded into history, not to return until the Neo-Classical movement of the early 20th century. The minuet is considerably different from the waltz, another famous dance in 3/4 time. The minuet generally has a slower, more deliberate tempo than a waltz, with a shortness of articulation on beats two or three leading to a strong downbeat. The articulations suggested in this edition attempt to create this minuet style.

## A Note on Teaching Order and Köchel Numbers

The pieces in this edition are presented in a suggested teaching order, with the works becoming progressively more difficult through the book. The pieces are identified by their Köchel or KV numbers (KV stands for Köchel-Verzeichnes, after the title of the original catalogue). Mozart's compositions were first catalogued by Ludwig Köchel, who published the first edition of his findings in 1862. The catalogue has undergone significant revisions, with the sixth and most recent edition appearing in 1964. In some cases, the composition dates of certain pieces have been changed due to continued Mozart research. As a result, a few pieces in this edition have two KV numbers. The first KV number is the original number from the first edition of the catalogue, and the second KV number is from the sixth edition.

## Notes on the Individual Pieces

### NANNERL'S NOTEBOOK

Mozart's older sister, Nannerl, began keyboard studies at age seven, when Wolfgang was three years old. She became an accomplished musician in her own right, and was a full participant in the musical tours the family took during the 1760s. Leopold Mozart gave her this notebook for practicing. It contained several pieces arranged in progressive order by contemporary composers, including Leopold Mozart himself. As a toddler Wolfgang was entranced by instruments and entertained himself by picking out intervals at the keyboard. By the time Mozart was four years old, he was learning to play some of the pieces in the notebook. Leopold Mozart notated in the pages when and how long it would take Wolfgang to master a particular piece. By the end of 1761, when Mozart was six years old, Leopold wrote down Wolfgang's first compositions as he played them. There is nothing crude about these early pieces; each is its own little jewel. There is a freshness of sound about them compared to other adult composers of the era. Amazingly, there is nothing immature about them.

### Minuet in F Major, KV 1d

This minuet is dated December 16, 1761 in Nannerl's Notebook and was composed in Salzburg. The form of the piece is AB, with repeats. This is a wonderful early work that has a gentile, song-like quality. The voice leading is perfect throughout. Voice leading refers to how individual voices interact across changing harmonies. Mozart uses very simple ideas, which still end up sounding like Mozart! Notice the deceptive cadence at measure 18: we expect the music to resolve to F major at this point, but

Mozart instead moves to D minor, delaying the final cadence to F major for a few more measures. We have realized the closing appoggiatura as a half note moving to a quarter note, imitating the phrase in measure 12.

### Minuet in F Major, KV 5

This piece is dated July 5, 1762, and was written in Salzburg. The form is AB, with repeats, and the two sections are very closely related in melodic and rhythmic material. Carefully observe the staccato articulation suggested in measure 3 on beat 2; this will give the performance the proper minuet lilt. Notice the abrupt change of texture that occurs from measure 4 into measure 5, and similarly from measure 14 into measure 15. The sections from measures 5 through 8, and again in measures 15 through 18, require the right hand to react quickly to the left hand, bouncing the sixteenth notes off of the main beats. Mozart again gives us a deceptive cadence in measure 20 before concluding the piece.

## THE LONDON NOTEBOOK

Wolfgang and Nannerl had a remarkable childhood, playing for the nobility throughout Europe, astonishing audiences wherever they went. The family embarked on trips to Munich (January 1762) and Vienna (October-December 1762) before going on an extensive European tour from June 1763 through November 1766. They spent time in over 80 cities, with lengthy stops in Brussels and Paris. Fifteen months of this tour were spent in London, from April 1764 through August 1765, their longest stay in any city on this vast journey. The young Wolfgang and his older sister Nannerl performed for all levels of aristocracy, with Wolfgang amazing audiences with his abilities to sight-read and improvise. Mozart met the composer Johann Christian Bach while in London, and his *style galant** music had a strong influence on Wolfgang's early compositions. While there is no evidence that J.C. Bach ever gave Mozart composition lessons, he certainly befriended the young composer, playing keyboard sonatas and improvising together.

The London Notebook, from which a few of the pieces in this collection are drawn, was a musical sketchbook that Mozart kept during his time in London. It is identified in the most recent Köchel catalogue as KV 15. Leopold Mozart was very ill during July and August of 1764, during which time all public performances were cancelled. It is possible that Wolfgang used this time to work in this notebook. It contains 43 pieces of varying levels of completeness. We see the young composer experimenting with phrase structure and extending his musical themes compared to his earlier compositions from *Nannerl's Notebook*. The pieces are sparsely ornamented in general, keeping in the *style galant* aesthetic of the times. Mozart explores the minor tonality extensively for the first time in this notebook. Even though these may have been compositional exercises, they feel like complete pieces. The music almost always has a playfulness about it. The notebook was dated 1764 on its cover, and modern scholarship believes that the pieces contained within were written either in 1764 or 1765.

*The *style galant* movement appeared in the early to mid-18th century as a reaction against the strict, contrapuntal music of the Baroque era, and was exemplified by composers such as Johann Christian Bach. Galant music is characterized by a lightness of texture, short phrases, and simple harmony with frequent cadences.

### Allegro in F Major, KV Anh. 109b, No. 1 (15a)

This happy little piece is written in ABA form, with repeats. It has the feeling of a fast minuet, and the tempo should be felt in one pulse per measure. Try practicing the piece slowly, at a more traditional minuet tempo before working up to a performance tempo. Notice which notes are marked staccato, and maintain that touch even if the other hand is playing a legato passage, as happens in measure 5.

### Minuet in G Major, KV 15y

This minuet is in ABA' form, with repeats. The return of the A section is abbreviated, with only the last six measures of the original section used to conclude the piece. This is a very courtly minuet, which is ornamented more than other similar pieces in the London Notebook. Utilizing stylish articulation is crucial to bringing this little gem to life. Always pay close attention to which notes are staccato and which notes are slurred and perform them accordingly.

## Rondo in F Major, KV 15hh

The form of this piece is ABACA, a simple rondo. A rondo is a piece in which the main theme returns multiple times in the tonic key. The piece feels like a brisk minuet, with the section in F minor serving as the Trio. Use a true portato touch in the first four measures, contrasting with a smooth legato for the next four measures. This contrast of articulation occurs constantly in this piece. Notice also the incredibly sophisticated harmonies Mozart uses in the F minor section, and how it is a stark contrast to the generally jovial spirit of the rest of the piece.

OTHER PIECES

## Andantino in E-flat Major, KV 236 (588b)

This piece is Mozart's adaptation of "Non vi turbate," an aria from Christoph Willibald Gluck's *Alceste*. It was probably written in 1783, possibly as a theme upon which variations would be based, though this has not been conclusively proven. Gluck was a major figure in Viennese and Parisian opera during the late 18th century, and *Alceste* had its premiere in Vienna on December 26, 1767. He later heavily revised the opera for performances in Paris in 1776. The aria on which this Andantino is based is from the original Vienna version. Mozart may have heard this aria in a performance of the opera given at Schönbrunn Castle in Vienna on December 3, 1781, which he mentions in a letter to his father from November 24 of the same year. Mozart's adaptation is in AB form, with repeats, and concentrates primarily on the orchestral introduction and conclusion to the aria. Find a singing tone for the top voice, remembering the origin of the piece.

## German Dance in C Major, KV 605, No. 3

This piece is an arrangement of one of the three German dances Mozart wrote for orchestra early in 1791, the last year of his life. This dance is for couples, and is performed in a quick 3/4 time. It became prominent in Germany and Austria during the late 18th century, with examples written by Haydn, Mozart, Beethoven, and Schubert. This dance form eventually evolved into the waltz. The form of this piece is ABCDAB, with repeats. When performing this music, remember its orchestral origins and produce a full, rounded tone. The repeated eighth notes should always have dynamic direction, with no two notes sounding the same. In the original version for orchestra, Mozart introduces sleigh bells in this Trio section. Make a significant contrast in dynamics and articulation in the "sleighride" Trio. The music should gently glide along, as a sleigh glides through the snow.

## Contradance in G Major, KV 269b

A contradance is a fast dance in 2/4 or 2/2 time, built upon repeated eight-measure phrases. Inspired by English peasant country dances, this form became popular with the European aristocracy during the late 17th and 18th centuries. Mozart wrote many such dances, as did Beethoven, in a set of 12 he published in 1802. This piece is dedicated to Count Johann Rudolf Graf Czernin, an amateur musician, and the nephew of the archbishop of Salzburg. Mozart was paid a yearly stipend to provide the Count with compositions, and this contradance is part of a set of dances composed for the Count in early 1777 in Salzburg. The form of this contradance is ABCD, with repeats, following closely the accepted structure of the dance. The second half of the concluding D section mirrors the conclusion of the A section. We suggest a *leggiero* touch in this piece, meaning light or nimble.

## Minuet in F Major, KV 6 (II)

This minuet comes from a Sonata in C Major that Wolfgang composed for keyboard with optional violin accompaniment (a popular genre at the time). The violin parts in compositions such as these were purely accompaniment, and the sonatas are satisfactorily performed by keyboard only. It was first published in February 1764 in Paris as Op. 1, No. 1, and was dedicated to Madame Victoire de France, the second daughter of the king of France. The Mozart family was staying in Paris at the time, seeking performances at court and for other nobility. The piece is in AB form, with repeats, with the end of the B section closely resembling the end of the A section. Mozart employs pedal points in this minuet, meaning that a particular tone is sustained as harmonies change around it. We see a pedal point on middle C in the first two measures in the top note of the left hand. It reappears in measures 5 through 8 on the left hand offbeats. Similar offbeat pedal points are found in the right hand in measures 11 through 14, and again in the left hand in measures 15 through 18.

### Adagio for Glass Harmonica, KV 356 (617a)

This haunting piece was written in early 1791 for Marianne Kirchgeßner, the nearly completely blind glass harmonica player, who gave the first performance of a version for glass harmonica, flute, oboe, violin, and cello on August 19, 1791 in Vienna. The glass harmonica uses a series of glass bowls or goblets to produce musical tones through friction. The sound produced is similar to when you run your finger along the moistened edge of a drinking glass. Benjamin Franklin invented a version of the glass harmonica in 1757, which he called an armonica. Other composers wrote works for the instrument, including Beethoven, Donizetti, Saint-Saëns, and Richard Strauss. This Adagio is in ABA' form, with the second appearance of the A section melodically embellished in the right hand. Notice that the entire piece is written in the treble register, and imagine the ethereal sound this instrument must have produced when you perform this on the piano. There is a gossamer quality to the piece, which must be performed with a profoundly smooth legato. While this glass harmonica was something of a novelty instrument, this composition is certainly not a novelty piece.

### Funeral March for Signor Maestro Contrapunto, KV 453a

This piece was written in Vienna in 1784. It was composed for Barbara Ployer, one of Mozart's students to whom he also dedicated his Piano Concerto in E-flat Major, KV 449 and his Piano Concerto in G Major, KV 453. It is in AB form, with repeats. Counterpoint, meaning the combination of two or more melodic lines, reached its zenith in terms of compositional popularity during the Baroque period. Its profuse use fell out of favor as the *style galant* movement took hold during the mid-18th century, and simpler, leaner music became more widespread. Barbara Ployer also took lessons from Mozart in music theory. This march, which lacks any counterpoint itself, is certainly a musical joke raised as a result of Ployer's lessons. It is still a beautifully conceived piece, in spite of its novelty. Performing this march requires a solemn-faced solemnity similar to an actor playing a very serious (and ultimately very ironic) role in a comedy. The piece is very dramatic, with many *subito* changes in dynamics. Taper the two-notes slurs carefully at the end of each main section.

### Rondo in C Major, KV 334 (320b)

This rondo is a piano arrangement of a movement from Mozart's "Divertimento in D Major" for strings and horns. It was most likely written during the summer of 1780 in Salzburg. A childhood friend of Mozart's, Georg Sigmund Robinig, graduated from the university that year, and it is likely that his family commissioned this Divertimento for a celebration of that occasion. This arrangement, possibly by the composer, is in ABABA form, a very simple rondo. We suggest articulations in this piece to imitate the orchestration of the original music. Imagine a violin playing the opening theme and how they would phrase and articulate that line. Be aware of the suggested dynamic changes and use them to dramatic effect, particularly when the main rondo theme returns each time.

### Piece for Clavier (Klavierstück) in F Major, KV 33B

This charming miniature was written in early October 1766 in Zurich. Mozart composed this piece on the back of minutes for a meeting of the Zurich Collegium Musicum. He likely performed the work on concerts held by the same organization on October 6 and 9, 1766. The form of this piece is ABA', with repeats, with the A section returning in abbreviated fashion in measure 19. This happy piece requires a light, bouncing touch in the broken octaves in the left hand. Notice how the first eight notes of the melody are developed and used to construct the rest of the piece.

### Contradance in D Major, KV 534

This contradance, subtitled "The Thunderstorm," was written in early 1788 as part of Mozart's newly acquired position of "Kammer-Musicus" (chamber musician) with the Viennese court. Among his responsibilities were to write dances for the carnival season. This piece (see the "Contradance in G Major" for a definition of "contradance") exists both in a version for orchestra and in two different arrangements for solo piano. The two versions for piano differ greatly—the first is based on the original manuscript and the second is based on the first published version. We have chosen to print the first version (based on the manuscript) in this edition. The orchestral version of this piece utilizes rare (for Mozart) instruments such as the piccolo and bass drum to describe this thunderstorm. The piece is through-composed and is an unusually rhapsodic and programmatic work for Mozart. One can imagine the distant rumblings of thunder at the beginning, which gradually draw closer during measures 9 through 16. The rain comes in measure 17 with the oscillating sixteenth notes in the right hand. There is a lull in the storm in measures 25 through 28 before it returns boisterously in measure 29. This is a truly Classical depiction of a thunderstorm, with the various musical sound effects never taken beyond the limits of good taste.

### Gavotte in F Major KV Anh. 10 (299b)

This gavotte is a piano arrangement of a movement from Mozart's only ballet, *Les petits riens*, composed in May and June 1778 in Paris. The ballet was first performed in Paris on June 11, 1778. A gavotte is a Baroque dance, usually in 2/4 or 2/2 time, with phrases that begin and end in the middle of a measure. The form of this piece is ABCA, with the C section (from measures 32 through 48) at partially related to the opening A section. It is a cheerful, bright dance, except for a brief detour to D minor in measures 41 through 48. The final A section is capped by a gracious coda. When practicing this piece, work to make the busy left hand passages as inconspicuous as possible. One could imagine leaping dancers in the very Gypsy-like passage in measures 9 and 10.

*—Elena Abend, editor*
*and Christopher Ruck, assistant editor*

## Notes

1. Marshall, Robert L. *Mozart Speaks: Views on Music, Musicians, and the World.* (New York: Schirmer Books, 1991), 202.

2. *Ibid.,* 196.

## Suggested Reading

Marshall, Robert L. *Mozart Speaks: Views on Music, Musicians, and the World.* New York: Schirmer Books, 1991.

Rosen, Charles. *The Classical Style: Haydn, Mozart, Beethoven.* exp. ed. New York: W. W. Norton, 1997.

Sadie, Stanley. *Mozart: The Early Years 1756-1781.* New York: W. W. Norton & Company, 2006.

Soloman, Maynard. *Mozart: A Life.* New York: HarperCollins, 1995.

Spaethling, Robert. *Mozart's Letters, Mozart's Life.* New York: W. W. Norton & Company, 2000.

# Andantino
## Adaptation of an aria* by Christoph Willibald Gluck

Wolfgang Amadeus Mozart
KV 236 (588b)

* "Non vi turbate" from Gluck's *Alceste.*

# Minuet

Wolfgang Amadeus Mozart
KV 1d

# German Dance

Wolfgang Amadeus Mozart
KV 605, No. 3

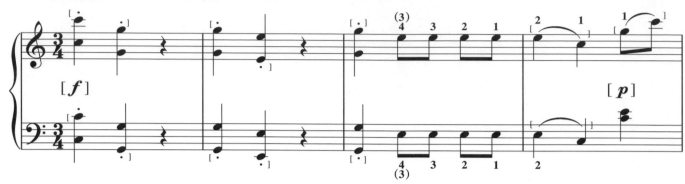

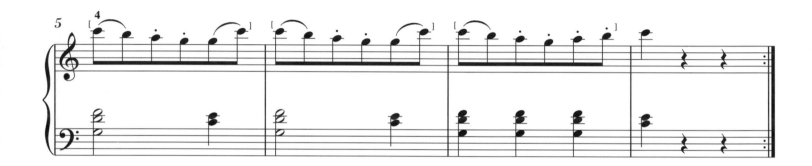

Eliminate repeats on the Da Capo.

**Trio (The Sleighride)**

**D.C. al Fine**
**second time**

# Minuet

Wolfgang Amadeus Mozart
KV 5

*for Johann Rudolf Graf Czernin*

# Contradance

Wolfgang Amadeus Mozart
KV 269b

# Minuet

Wolfgang Amadeus Mozart
KV 6 (II)

# Adagio for Glass Harmonica

Wolfgang Amadeus Mozart
KV 356 (617a)

# Funeral March for Signor Maestro Contrapunto

Wolfgang Amadeus Mozart
KV 453a

# Allegro

Wolfgang Amadeus Mozart
KV Anh. 109b, No. 1 (15a)

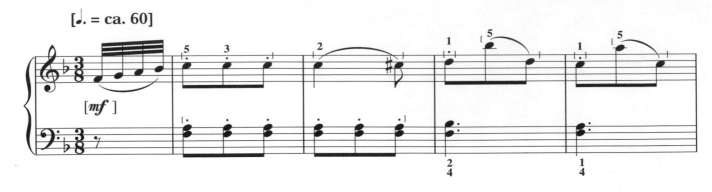

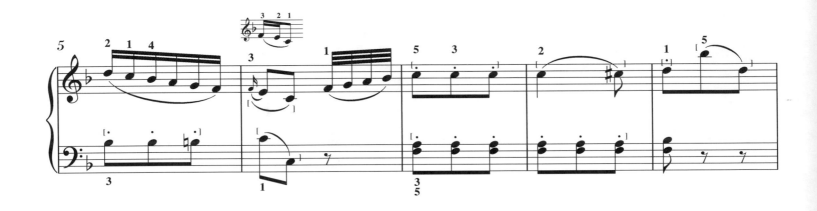

# Minuet

Wolfgang Amadeus Mozart
KV 15y

# Rondo

Wolfgang Amadeus Mozart
KV 334 (320b)

# Piece for Clavier
## (Klavierstück)

Wolfgang Amadeus Mozart
KV 33B

[ *poco rit. 2nd time* ]

# Contradance
## The Thunderstorm

Wolfgang Amadeus Mozart
KV 534

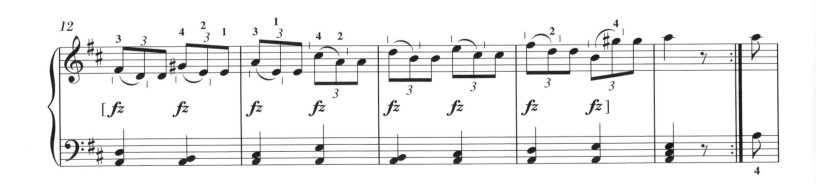

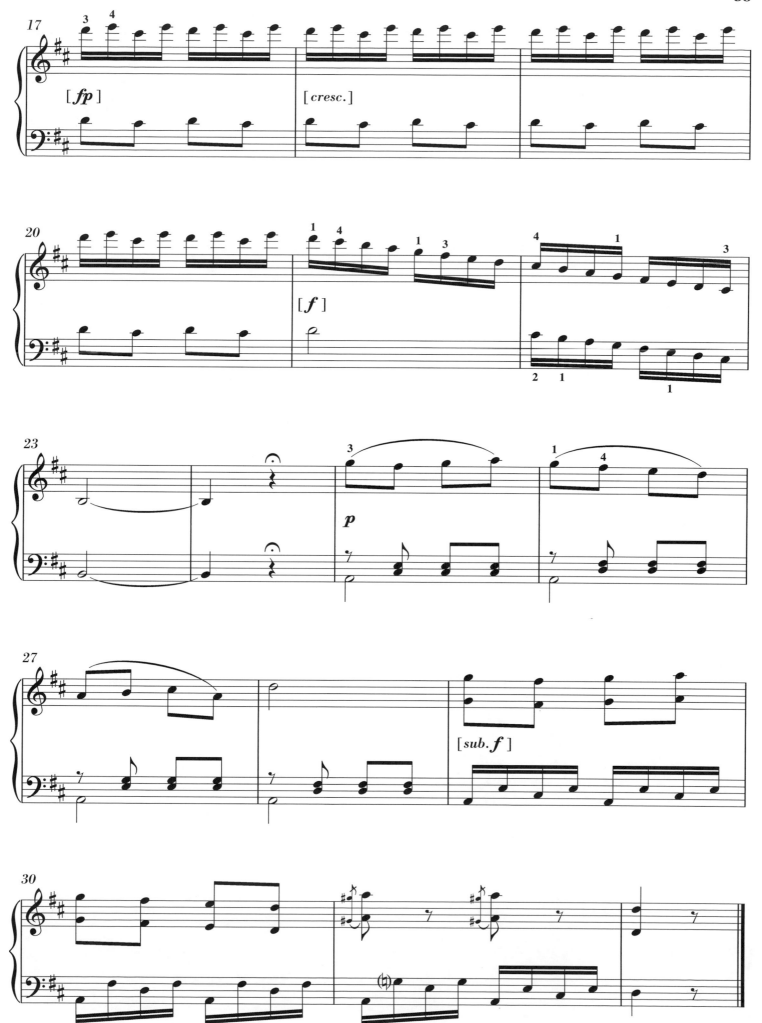

# Gavotte
## from *Les petits riens*

Wolfgang Amadeus Mozart
KV Anh. 10 (299b)

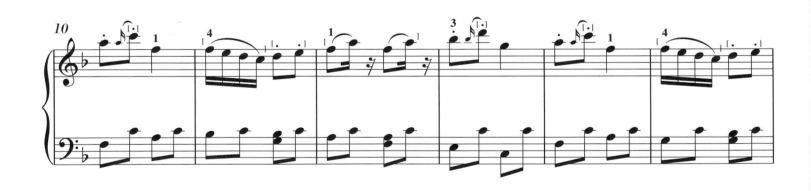

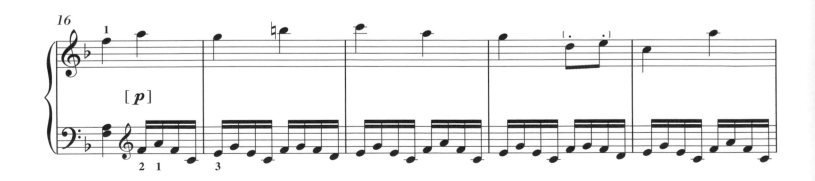

# Rondo

Wolfgang Amadeus Mozart
KV 15hh

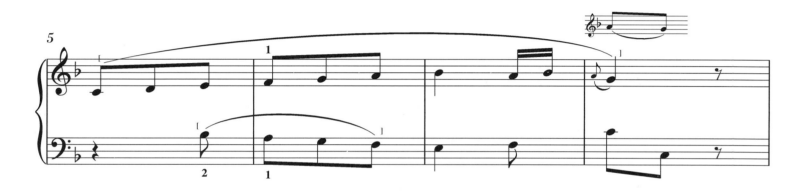

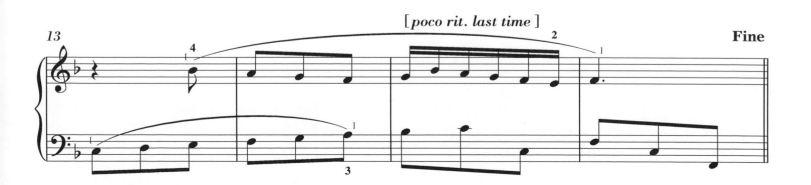

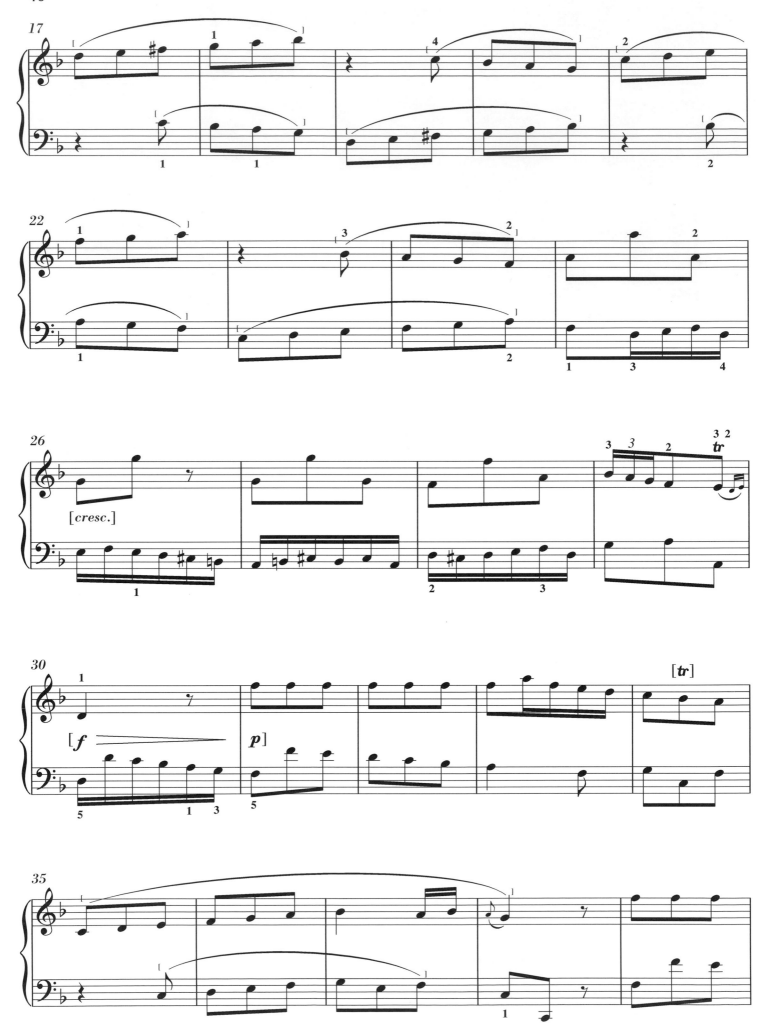

D.C. al Fine

# ABOUT THE EDITOR

## ELENA ABEND

Born in Caracas, Venezuela, pianist Elena Abend is well known as a soloist and chamber musician. She has performed with all the major orchestras of her country and has recorded with the Filarmonica Nacional. As the recipient of a scholarship from the Venezuelan Council for the Arts, Abend studied at the Juilliard School, where she received her Bachelor and Master degrees. She has performed at the Purcell Room in London's Royal Festival Hall, Avery Fisher Hall in New York's Lincoln Center, Weill Recital Hall at Carnegie Hall and the Academy of Music with the Philadelphia Orchestra. Other engagements have included the Wigmore Hall in London, the Toulouse Conservatoire in France, the Corcoran Gallery in Washington DC, the United Nations, Merkin Concert Hall in New York, Chicago Cultural Center, the Pabst Theater in Milwaukee, the Atlanta Historical Society, the Teresa Carreno Cultural Center in Caracas, as well as the Theatre Luxembourg in Meaux, France. Other chamber music collaborations include numerous performances at the Ravinia and Marlboro Music Festivals, as well as live broadcasts on Philadelphia's WFLN, The Dame Myra Hess Concert Series on Chicago's WFMT and Wisconsin Public Radio at the Chazen Museum in Madison, Wisconsin. Abend has been on the Faculty of the Wisconsin Conservatory of Music, Indiana University's String Academy summer program and the Milwaukee Chamber Music Festival. She has also performed on the Milwaukee Chamber Orchestra Series at Schwan Concert Hall, Piano Chamber, New Generations, Music from Almost Yesterday and the Yolanda Marculescu Vocal Art Series at the University of Wisconsin. She has performed with the "Rembrandt Chamber Players" of Chicago, "Present Music Now," "Frankly Music," and the Fine Arts Quartet on several occasions. A newly released CD with clarinetist Todd Levy, performing the two Brahms Sonatas and the Schumann Fantasy and Romance pieces, is now available on the Avie label. She has also recorded extensively for the *Schirmer Instrumental Library* series for G. Schirmer. She is on the music faculty at the University of Wisconsin-Milwaukee.